THE CHANDLER

A COMEDY IN THREE ACTS

BY

ALFRED DE MUSSET

(Published in 1835; Produced in 1848).

DONE INTO ENGLISH BY
DR. EDMUND BURKE THOMPSON

(1905.)

Edited by
B. K. De Fabris

Timeless📖Classics

CHARACTERS

M. ANDRÉ, *a Notary.*
JACQUELINE, *his Wife.*
CLAVAROCHE, *Officer of Dragoons.*
FORTUNIO, *A Clerk.*
GUILLAUME, A *Clerk.*
LANDRY, *A Clerk.*
MADELON, *A Servant.*
PIERRE, *A Gardener.*

A Small City.

ACT THE FIRST

SCENE I

(A bedroom. Jacqueline, in bed. Enter M. André, in dressing-gown.)

ANDRÉ. Hallo, wife! hey, Jacqueline! hey! hallo! Jacqueline! Wife! Plague take the sleepy-head! Hey! hey! wife, wake up! Hallo! hallo! get up, Jacqueline! How she sleeps! Hallo! hallo! hallo! hey! hey! hey! wife! wife! wife! It's I, André, your husband, who has something serious to say to you. Hey! hey! Jacqueline, are you dead? If you don't wake up right away, I'll throw a pitcher of water on you!

JACQUELINE. What is it, love?

ANDRÉ. Light of my life, it isn't anything very bad. Will you stop stretching? Sleeping is a business with you. Listen to me, I have something to say to you. Last night, Landry, my clerk...

JACQUELINE. But, good gracious! it isn't morning. Are you getting crazy, André, to wake me up like this without any reason? For goodness' sake, go back to bed! Are you ill?

ANDRÉ. I am neither crazy nor ill, and I awaken you for a very good reason. I want to talk to you now; try to listen to me, in the first place, and afterward to reply to me. This is what happened to Landry, my clerk; you know who he is...

JACQUELINE. What time is it, if you please?

ANDRÉ. It is six o'clock in the morning. Pay attention to what I am saying to you; it is not a joking matter, and I am not accustomed to jokes. My honor, yours, and the lives of both of us, perhaps, depend upon the explanation which I am about to make to you. Landry, my clerk, saw, last night...

JACQUELINE. But, André, if you are sick, you must tell me so right away. Is not it my place, sweetheart, to take care of you and watch over you?

ANDRÉ. I'm all right, I tell you. Are you in a mood to listen to me?

JACQUELINE. Ah, my God! you frighten me. Has anybody been robbing us?

ANDRÉ. No, nobody has been robbing us. Sit there, in your bed, and listen to me attentively. Landry, my clerk, came to awaken me, to return a certain piece of work which he had to finish last night. As he was in my office...

JACQUELINE. Ah, holy Virgin! I know. You must have had some quarrel at the cafe where you go?

ANDRÉ. No, no, I haven't had any quarrel, and nothing has happened to me. Will you listen to me? I tell you that Landry, my clerk, saw a man slip in at your window last night.

JACQUELINE. I guess by your face that you have lost at gambling.

ANDRÉ. Ah, come, wife, are you deaf? You have a lover, madame; is that plain enough? You are deceiving me. A man scaled our walls last night. What does that mean?

JACQUELINE. Be kind enough to open the shutter.

ANDRÉ. There, it is open. You can yawn after dinner. Thank God, you scarcely fail there! Beware, Jacqueline! I am a man of a peaceable disposition, and I have taken good care of you. I was your father's friend, and you are almost as much my daughter as my wife. I resolved, in coming here, to treat you kindly; and you see that I am doing so, since, before condemning you, I wish to confide in you, and give you a chance to defend yourself, and to explain yourself categorically. If you refuse, beware! There's a garrison in the city, and you see, God forgive me! a great many hussars. Your silence might confirm the suspicions which I have entertained for a long time.

JACQUELINE. Ah, André, you don't love me any more! It is useless for you to conceal the mortal coldness which has replaced so much love, beneath friendly words. It did not use to be so; you did not use to talk to me like this; you would not once have condemned me upon a word, without hearing me. Two years of peace, of love and happiness, would not have been, upon a single word, dissipated like a shadow. But then, jealousy prompts you to it; for a long time a cold indifference has opened the door of your heart to that. Of what use would evidence be? Innocence itself would be wrong in your eyes. You do not love me any longer, since you accuse me.

ANDRÉ. How silly you are, Jacqueline! It isn't a question of that. Landry, my clerk, saw a man...

JACQUELINE. Ah, my God! I heard well enough. Do you take me for a brute, that you din it into my head like this? You tire me to death.

ANDRÉ. What's the reason that you do not answer me?

JACQUELINE *(weeping)*. Merciful heavens, how unhappy I am! Whatever will become of me? I see very plainly that you have resolved upon my death; you can do whatever you please with me; you are a man, and I am a woman; the strength is on your side. I am resigned; I expected this; you seize upon the first pretext to justify your violence. There is nothing left for me but to go away from here. I will go with my child into a convent, into a desert, if it is possible; I will carry with me there, I will bury in my heart, the memory of times forever past.

ANDRÉ. Wife! wife! for the love of God and all the saints, are you making a fool of me?

JACQUELINE. Ah, come! in earnest, André, is it serious what you say?

ANDRÉ. Is what I say serious? Good heavens! I am getting out of patience, and I don't know what stops me from taking you into court.

JACQUELINE. You—into court?

ANDRÉ. Yes, into court. It's enough to drive a man wild, to have anything to do with such a mule. I never heard of any one being so obstinate.

JACQUELINE *(springing out of bed)*. You saw a man enter by the window? Did you see him, yes or no?

ANDRÉ. I did not see him with my own eyes.

JACQUELINE. You did not see him with your own eyes, and you want to take me into court?

ANDRÉ. Yes, by heavens! if you do not answer me.

JACQUELINE. Do you know one thing, André, that my grand-mother learned from hers? When a husband trusts his wife, he keeps his insults for her sake, and when he is sure of his facts, he does not want to consult her. When a man has suspicions, he raises them; when a man lacks proof, he keeps still; and when a man can not demonstrate that he is right, he is wrong. Well, come along; let us get out of here.

ANDRÉ. So that is the way you take it?

JACQUELINE. Yes, that is the way. Go on, I will follow you.

ANDRÉ. And where would you have me go at this hour?

JACQUELINE. To court.

ANDRÉ. But, Jacqueline ...

JACQUELINE. Go on; go on. When one threatens, it is not necessary to threaten in vain.

ANDRÉ. Nonsense! Come, calm yourself a little.

JACQUELINE. No; you wish to take me to court, and I want to go there at once.

ANDRÉ. What will you say in your defense? You can just as well tell me now.

JACQUELINE. No, I don't ' want to say anything here.

ANDRÉ. Why?

JACQUELINE. Because I want to go to court.

ANDRÉ. You are enough to drive me crazy, and it seems to me that I am dreaming. Eternal God, Creator of the world, this thing will make me sick! Why? what? is it possible? I was in my bed; I was sleeping, and I call upon the walls to witness that it was with all my might. Landry, my clerk, a child of sixteen, who never spoke ill of anybody in his life, the most truthful boy in the world, who had spent the night in copying an inventory, sees a man enter the window; he tells me about it; I put on my dressing-gown, I come to find you in friendship, I ask you, for God's sake, to explain to me what it means, and you abuse me! You fly into a passion, to the extent of springing out of bed and seizing me by the throat! No, this beats anything I ever heard of. I shall not be fit for anything for a week. Jacqueline, my little wife, it is you who treats me like this!

JACQUELINE. Go on; go on; you are a poor, abused man.

ANDRÉ. But after all, my dear, what harm would it do you to answer me? Do you believe that I would think that you are really deceiving me? Alas, my God, a word from you would suffice. Why do you not want to say it? Perhaps it was some thief who slipped in at our window. This neighborhood is not of the safest, and we should do well to change it. All these soldiers are very disagreeable to me, my beauty, my jewel! When we go for a walk, to the theater, to a ball, and even at home, these men never leave us alone. I can not say a word in your ear without running foul of their epaulets, and getting their great hooked sabers tangled up with my legs. Who knows whether their impertinence would not go to the extent of entering our windows? You know nothing about it, I see plainly; it is not you that encourages them. Those rascals are capable of anything. Come, now! shake hands. Are you angry with me, Jacqueline?

JACQUELINE. Of course I am angry with you. The idea of your threatening to take me into court! When my mother knows it, she will give it to you!

ANDRÉ. Ah, my child, don't tell her. What's the use of mixing others into our little disagreements? They are passing clouds which obscure the sun for a moment, only to leave it brighter than before.

JACQUELINE. All right! Give me your hand.

ANDRÉ. Do I not know that you love me? Have I not the most implicit confidence in you? Have you not given me every earthly proof, for the past two years, that you are devoted to me, Jacqueline?

8

This window, of which Landry speaks, does not open directly into your chamber; by crossing the inner court, you go from there to the vegetable garden. I should not be surprised if our neighbor, M. Pierre, comes to poach from my trellises. That will not do! I will have the Gardener watch to-night, and set a trap in the alley. We shall have a good laugh over it to-morrow.

JACQUELINE. I am tired to death, and you have awakened me at this unearthly hour.

ANDRÉ. Go to bed again, darling. I am off. I will leave you now. Good-by; let us think no more about it. You see, my child, I do not make the least search in your apartment; I have not opened a closet; I take your word for it. It seems to me that I love you a hundred times more for having wrongfully suspected you and found you innocent. I will make up for it, by and by. We will go to the country, and I will make you a nice present. Good-by, good-by; I will see you later. *(Exit.)*

(Jacqueline, alone, opens a Closet; Captain Clavaroche is seen cowering there.)

CLAVAROCHE *(coming out of the closet)*. Faugh!

JACQUELINE. Quick, go away! My husband is jealous. Somebody saw you but did not recognize you. You can not come here again. How did you get along in there?

CLAVAROCHE. First-rate.

JACQUELINE. We have no time to lose; what shall we do? We must meet, without letting anybody see us. What shall we decide upon? The Gardener will be on the watch tonight. I do not altogether trust my maid. We must go somewhere else; it's impossible to meet here. Everything is known in a small town. You are covered with dust, and I believe you limp.

CLAVAROCHE. I bruised my knee and my head. The hilt of my sword jammed into my ribs. Poh! one would think I had come out of a gristmill.

JACQUELINE. Burn my letters when you get home. If anybody were to find them, I should be ruined; my mother would send me to a convent. Landry, a clerk, saw you getting in at the window; he shall pay me for that. What's to be done? Is there any way? Tell me! You are as pale as death.

CLAVAROCHE. I was in a cramped position when you pushed the door to, so that, for more than an hour, I was like a specimen of natural history in a bottle of alcohol.

JACQUELINE. Well, let us see—what shall we do?

CLAVAROCHE. Nonsense! there's nothing so easy as that.

JACQUELINE. What then?

CLAVAROCHE. I do not know; but nothing is easier. Do you think this is my first scrape? I am all used up; give me a glass of water.

JACQUELINE. I believe the best thing would be to meet each other at the farmhouse.

CLAVAROCHE. These husbands, when their suspicions are aroused, are troublesome creatures. This uniform is in a pretty state, and I shall be a pretty sight on parade! *(He takes a drink.)* Have you a brush here? The devil take me, if with all this dust I did not have hard work to keep from sneezing!

JACQUELINE. Here are my toilet articles: take whatever you want.

CLAVAROCHE *(brushing his hair.)* What's the use of going to the farm-house? Your husband is, on the whole, of a mild disposition. Is it a habit of his to have these nocturnal visions?

JACQUELINE. No, thank God! I am trembling yet on account of it. But you must remember that with the ideas that he has in his head now, all his suspicions will fall upon you.

CLAVAROCHE. Why upon me?

JACQUELINE. Why? But... I do not know... It seems to me that it will be so. Bless me! Clavaroche, truth is a queer thing; it is something like a specter: you feel its presence without being able to put your finger on it.

CLAVAROCHE *(adjusting his uniform).* Bah! only old fogies and lawyers say that everything is known. They have a good reason for that, which is, that anything that is unknown is ignored, and consequently does not exist. I seem to be talking nonsense. Think it over, you will find that it is true.

JACQUELINE. Just as you like. I am trembling like a leaf, and I am scared to death.

CLAVAROCHE. Be patient; we shall contrive something.

JACQUELINE. How? Go, it is daylight.

CLAVAROCHE. Ah, good heavens, how silly you are! You are as pretty as a picture with your great frightened look. Let me think a minute; sit down there, and let us consider the situation. See, I am almost presentable, and in good order again. Hard-hearted closet that you have there! It does not do your clothes a bit of good.

JACQUELINE. Do not laugh; you make me shudder.

CLAVAROCHE. Well, my dear, I will tell you my rules of conduct. When you cross the path of that species of malignant beast called a jealous husband.

JACQUELINE. Ah, Clavaroche, for my sake!

CLAVAROCHE. Have I shocked you? *(He kisses her.)*

JACQUELINE. At least, speak lower.

CLAVAROCHE. There are three sure means of avoiding all inconvenience. The first is to separate; but that we scarcely want to do.

JACQUELINE. You will frighten me to death.

CLAVAROCHE. The second, and incontestably the best, is to pay no attention to it, and, if necessity arises.

JACQUELINE. Well?

CLAVAROCHE. No, that is not any better either; you have a husband who wields the pen; the sword must be kept in the scabbard. There remains, then, the third, which is, to find a "chandler."

JACQUELINE. A chandler? What do you mean?

CLAVAROCHE. That's what we call, in the regiment, a tall, good-looking young fellow, whose duty it is to carry a shawl or a parasol at need; who, when a lady arises to dance, goes gravely and seats himself in her chair, and follows her through the crowd with a melancholy eye, while toying with her fan; who gives her his hand to assist her from her box at the opera, and proudly returns to the buffet the glass from which she has just been drinking; he accompanies her upon her walks, reads to her in the evening, and buzzes about her incessantly, besieging her ear with a shower of silly nothings. If anybody admires the lady, he bridles up, and if anybody insults her he fights. If a cushion is needed for the sofa, it is he who hastens to search for it, for he knows the house in all its parts, he forms a part of the furniture, and goes about the corridors without a light. He plays cribbage and piquet with the aunts of an evening. As he circumvents the husband by clever and ready tactics, he presently gets himself disliked. If anything is going on anywhere to which the lady wishes to go, he is up by daybreak, by noon he is at the place or on the road, and he has marked the seats with his gloves. Ask him why he has made himself her shadow, he does not know and can not tell. Is it not because the lady sometimes encourages him with a smile, and abandons her fingers to him in waltzing, while he squeezes them with rapture. He is like these great lords who hold an honorary position and the entrée on high days and holidays; but the private office is closed to them; they have no business there. In short, his favors end where the true ones begin; he has all that anybody sees of women, and nothing that one desires of them. Behind this convenient puppet hides the happy mystery; he serves as a screen to all that is going on clandestinely. If the husband is jealous, it is of him. Is there idle talk? It is on his account. It is he that gets put out of the door some fine morning, when the valets have heard footsteps in madame's apartment during the night; it is he that is spied upon in secret; his letters, full of respect and tenderness, are opened by the mother-in-law; he goes and comes, he is restless, he is allowed to bear the brunt, it is his business; by means of him, the discreet lover and the very innocent lady, covered with an impenetrable disguise, laugh at him and the lookers-on.

JACQUELINE. I can not help laughing, in spite of the fact that I do not want to. And why does this person have the odd name of "chandler "?

CLAVAROCHE. Ah, but! it's because it is he who carries the …

JACQUELINE. That's right, that's right; I understand you.

CLAVAROCHE. Think, my dear: among your friends, have you not some good soul capable of filling this important position, who, with good faith, is agreeable? Seek look think of that. *(He looks at his watch.)* Seven o'clock! I must leave you. I am on duty to-day.

JACQUELINE. But, Clavaroche, indeed, I know nobody here; and besides, it is a deception for which I should not have the courage. What! encourage a young man, attract him to you, allow him to hope, perhaps make him fall in love with you in earnest, and make a jest of what he may suffer? It's a wanton thing that you propose to me.

CLAVAROCHE. Would you rather I should lose you? And in our present embarrassment, do you not see that we must ward off suspicion at any price?

JACQUELINE. Why make them fall upon another?

CLAVAROCHE. Ah, they will fall. Suspicions, my dear, the suspicions of a jealous husband, can not soar in space; they are not swallows. They must light sooner or later, and the safest thing is to prepare a place for them.

JACQUELINE. No, decidedly, I can not. Would it not be necessary to compromise myself very truly for that?

CLAVAROCHE. Are you joking? Would you not always be able to demonstrate your innocence if necessity arises? A lover is not a paramour!

JACQUELINE. Very well ... but time is pressing. Whom do you want? Mention somebody to me.

CLAVAROCHE *(at the window)*. Look here! here, in your court, are three young men sitting at the foot of a tree; they are your husband's clerks. I leave you the choice between them. When I return, let one of them be madly in love with you.

JACQUELINE. How would that be possible? I never spoke to them in my life.

CLAVAROCHE. Are you not a daughter of Eve! Come, Jacqueline, consent.

JACQUELINE. Do not count upon it; I shall do nothing of the kind.

CLAVAROCHE. Give me your hand; thanks. Good-by, my very timid little blond; you are clever, young, and pretty, in love ... a little, are you not, madame? To the task! good luck!

JACQUELINE. You are bold, Clavaroche.

CLAVAROCHE. Proud and bold; proud of pleasing you; and bold to keep you. *(Exit.)*

SCENE II

(A little garden. Fortunio, Landry, and Guillaume, seated.)

FORTUNIO. Really, that is singular, and this adventure is strange.

LANDRY. Do not go and prattle about it, at least; you would make me lose my place.

FORTUNIO. Very strange and very admirable. Yes, whoever he may be, he is a lucky man.

LANDRY. Promise me to say nothing about it. André made me swear too.

GUILLAUME. You must not open your mouth concerning your neighbor, the king, or women.

FORTUNIO. It rejoices my heart that such things exist. You really saw that, Landry?

LANDRY. That's right; there is not any doubt about it.

FORTUNIO. You heard stealthy footsteps?

LANDRY. Like a cat's, behind the wall.

FORTUNIO. The window creak softly?

LANDRY. Like a grain of sand under the foot.

FORTUNIO. Then the shadow of a man upon the wall, when he had jumped over the back gate?

LANDRY. Like a specter, in his mantle.

FORTUNIO. And a hand behind the shutter?

LANDRY. Trembling like a leaf.

FORTUNIO. A light in the gallery, then a kiss, then a few distant footsteps?

LANDRY. Then silence, the curtains drawn, and the light disappeared.

FORTUNIO. If I had been in your place, I should have stayed until daylight.

GUILLAUME. Are you in love with Jacqueline? That would have been a pretty trick!

FORTUNIO. I swear before God, Guillaume, that I have never raised my eyes in Jacqueline's presence. I should not dare to love her, even in a dream. I attended a ball once where she was; my hand did not touch hers; she never opened her lips to me. I have never known anything in my life of what she does or what she thinks, except that she walks here afternoons, and I have breathed upon our window panes to look at her walking in the path.

GUILLAUME. If you are not in love with her, why do you say that you would have remained? There was nothing better to do than just what Landry did: to go and tell the thing frankly to André, our employer.

FORTUNIO. Landry did as he pleased. Let Romeo have his Juliet! I should like to be the little bird to warn them of danger.

GUILLAUME. There you are with your pranks! What good would it do you if Jacqueline has a lover? It is some officer of the garrison.

FORTUNIO. I should like to have been in the office; I should like to have seen all that.

GUILLAUME. Bless me; our bookseller is poisoning you with his romances. What could you profit by this affair—to be Jack Sprat, as before? Perhaps you hope that you may have your turn. Oh, yes, doubtless, my gentleman imagines that she will think of him some day. Poor boy! you scarcely know our fine country ladies. We, with our black coats, are nothing but rubbish, more or less fit for seamstresses. They have no use for anything that does not wear red trousers, and once their conquest is made, what matters it if the garrison changes! All soldiers resemble one another. Who loves one of them, loves a hundred. Only the lapels of the coats are changed, and yellow becomes green or white. For the rest, don't they find the same curl of the mustache again, the same manner of the guardsman, the same language, and the same pleasure? They are all made after one pattern; they might deceive themselves at a pinch.

FORTUNIO. There is no use of talking with you; you pass your holidays and Sundays in watching ball games.

GUILLAUME. And you, all alone at your window, your nose poked into your nosegays. That's a great difference! You will become raving mad with your romantic notions. Come, let us go in; what are you thinking of? It is time to go to work.

FORTUNIO. I wish I had been with Landry in the office last night.

(Exeunt. Enter Jacqueline and her servant.)

JACQUELINE. Our plums are going to be fine this year, and our arbors look well. Come over here a little while, and let us sit down upon this bench.

MADELON. Is madame not afraid of taking cold? It is not very warm this morning.

JACQUELINE. Indeed, I believe that I have never been twice in this part of the garden, in all the two years that I have lived in this house. Look at this honeysuckle vine! These trellises are well-arranged for climbing plants.

MADELON. For all that, madame has no hat on; she wished to come out bare-headed.

JACQUELINE. Tell me, since you are here: who are those young men in the lower room? Can I be mistaken? I believe they are looking at us; they were here just now.

MADELON. Madame does not know them! They are M. André's clerks.

JACQUELINE. Ah! do you know them, Madelon? You seem to blush as you say that.

MADELON. I, madame, why should I? I know them from seeing them every day; I don't know that I know them.

JACQUELINE. Come, confess that you blushed. And, in fact, why should you deny it? As far as I can see from here, those boys are not so bad. Come, confide in me a little, which one do you prefer? You are a pretty girl, Madelon; what harm if these young men do flirt with you?

MADELON. I do not say that there is any harm; those young men are nice enough, and their families are respectable. One of them is a short blond; the grisettes of the Boulevard do not turn their noses up at a tip of his hat.

JACQUELINE *(approaching the house)*. Which? The one with the mustache?

MADELON. Oh, my, no! That's M. Landry, a great, lanky fellow who never knows what to say.

JACQUELINE. The one that is writing there?

MADELON. No, not at all; that's M. Guillaume, a nice, steady fellow; but his hair does not curl, and he is to be pitied when he tries to dance of a Sunday.

JACQUELINE. Of whom are you speaking then? I do not think there are any others besides those in the office.

MADELON. Do you not see that nice, well-dressed young man at the window? Look! he is bending down; that's young Fortunio.

JACQUELINE. Yes, indeed, now I see him. He looks very well, upon my word, with his hair over his ears and his little innocent air. Beware, Madelon; those angels lead young girls astray. And that young gentleman, with his blue eyes, flirts with grisettes, does he? Well, Madelon, it is not necessary to drop yours in such a peculiar manner because of that. Really, you might make a worse choice. That one knows what to say, I suppose, and is a master hand at dancing?

MADELON. Saving the respect due to you, madame, if I were to believe him in love, here, it would not be with such an insignificant person as I. If you had but turned your head when you were passing among the trees, you would have seen him more than once, with his arms folded, his pen behind his ear, looking at you with all his eyes.

JACQUELINE. Are you joking, miss, and do you know whom you are talking to?

MADELON. A cat may look at a king, and there are people who say that the king likes to be looked at. He is not such a fool, that boy, and his father is a rich goldsmith. I don't think it is any insult to look at people when they pass.

JACQUELINE. Who told you that it is I at whom he looks? I imagine that he has not made a confidant of you in the matter.

MADELON. Come, madame! When a young man turns his head, it is hardly necessary to be a woman not to guess which way he is looking. I do not want his confidence, and nobody told me what I know about it.

JACQUELINE. I am cold. Go and find me a shawl, and spare me your idle talk.

(Exit the servant.)

JACQUELINE. If I am not mistaken, it is the gardener whom I noticed among those trees. Hallo! Pierre, listen.

THE GARDENER *(entering)*. Did you call me, madame?

JACQUELINE. Yes. Go in there; ask for a clerk called Fortunio. Tell him to come here; I have something to say to him.

(Exit gardener. A moment later enter Fortunio.)

FORTUNIO. Madame, it is doubtless a mistake; I was told that you had asked for me.

JACQUELINE. Sit down; it is not a mistake. You see me, M. Fortunio, greatly embarrassed, greatly distressed. I do not exactly know how to say what I have to ask of you, nor why I appeal to you.

FORTUNIO. I am only the third clerk; if it pertains to some important business, Guillaume, our head clerk, is there. Do you wish me to call him?

JACQUELINE. No, indeed. If it were a business matter, have I not my husband?

FORTUNIO. Can I be of any use? Please speak with confidence. Although I am very young, I would gladly die to be of service to you.

JACQUELINE. That is gallantly and valiantly spoken; and yet, if I am not mistaken, I am unknown to you.

FORTUNIO. The star that shines on the horizon knows not the eyes which regard it; but it is known to the least herdsman who walks on the hillside.

JACQUELINE. It is a secret that I have to tell you, and I hesitate for two reasons: in the first place, you might betray me; and in the second place, even in serving me you might get a bad opinion of me.

FORTUNIO. May I submit myself to the proof? I beg you to believe in me.

JACQUELINE. But, as you say, you are very young. You might believe in yourself, and not always answer for it.

FORTUNIO. You are more beautiful than I am young; what my heart feels, I answer for.

JACQUELINE. Necessity is imprudent. See if anybody is listening.

17

FORTUNIO. No one; the garden is empty, and I closed the door to the office.

JACQUELINE. No, decidedly I can not do it. Pardon me for this useless proceeding, and say no more about it.

FORTUNIO. Alas! Madame, I am very unfortunate! But just as you please about it.

JACQUELINE. The position that I am in is somewhat peculiar. I have need—shall I confess it to you?—not exactly of a friend, but of the kindly offices of a friend. I do not know what to decide. I was walking here in the garden, looking at these trellises; and I tell you, I do not know why, I saw you at that window, and the idea came to me to send for you.

FORTUNIO. Whatever the caprice of fortune to which I owe this favor, permit me to profit by it. I can only repeat my own words: I would willingly die for you.

JACQUELINE. Don't repeat them too often to me; that's the surest way of making me keep still.

FORTUNIO. Why? It's from the bottom of my heart...

JACQUELINE. Why? why? You don't know anything about it, and I simply do not want to think about it. No; what I have to ask of you could not have such serious consequences. Thank God! it is nothing —a trifling thing. You are a child, are you not? You think me pretty, perhaps, and you thoughtlessly pay me a few compliments. I accept them as such, it's quite natural; any man in your place might say as much.

FORTUNIO. Madame, I have never told an untruth. It is very true that I am a child, and one might doubt my words; but such as they are, God can judge them.

JACQUELINE. All right; you know your part, and you won't go back upon your word. Enough of that. Take this seat, and make yourself comfortable.

FORTUNIO. I will do it to please you.

JACQUELINE. Pardon me for a question which may seem strange to you. Madelon, my maid, told me that your father was a jeweler. He must happen to be connected with the merchants of the city, is he not?

FORTUNIO. Yes, madame, I may say that there are very few who do not know our house.

JACQUELINE. Consequently you have occasion to go about the business section, and your face is known in the stores of the Boulevard?

FORTUNIO. Yes, madame, at your service.

JACQUELINE. A lady of my acquaintance has a husband who is stingy and jealous. She does not lack for money, but she can not spend it. Her pleasures, her tastes, her dress, her whims, if you please (for what woman lives without them?), everything is regulated and controlled. It is not that at the end of the year she has to economize; but each month, almost each week, she must count, discuss, calculate everything she buys. You understand that moralizing, all the sermons of economy possible, all the reasons of a miser, are not lacking upon occasion; in short, with ample means, she leads the most uncomfortable kind of a life. She is as poor as a church mouse, and her money is no use to her. He who speaks of dress, in speaking of women, speaks upon a very important subject, you know. So it is necessary to resort to some stratagem, at any price. Trades-people only bear in mind those commonplace expenditures which the husband calls "of prime necessity; " these things are satisfactory ordinarily; but, on certain fitting occasions, certain other secret memoranda make mention of a few trifles which the wife, in her turn, calls "of the second necessity," which is the real one, and which unreasonable minds call superfluities. Considering that, all is arranged admirably; each one can have his own account, and the husband, sure of his receipts, does not know enough about clothes to suspect that he has not paid for all that he sees upon his wife's back.

FORTUNIO. I see no great harm in that.

JACQUELINE. Now, then, this is what has happened: the husband, a little suspicious, has ended by noticing not to many clothes, but too little money. He has threatened the servants, thumped upon his cashbox, and scolded the merchants. The poor miserable wife has not lost a farthing of it; but she finds herself, like a new Tantalus, devoured from morning to night by a longing for clothes. No more confidants, no more secret accounts, no more unknown expenditures. This longing torments her, however; she seeks to satisfy it at any hazard. She needs some clever young man, discreet, above all things, and of sufficient prominence in the city not to arouse any suspicion, to go to the stores and buy, as for himself, such things as she wants and has need of. In the first place, it must be some one who has free access to the house, so that he can come and go with confidence, some one who has good taste, of course, and knows how to make wise selections. Perhaps it might be a happy chance if there were in the town, some pretty, coquettish girl, to whom it was known that he was paying attention. That is not the case with you, I suppose? That chance would justify everything. It would then be supposed that the purchases were made for the lady-love. This is what it is necessary to find.

FORTUNIO. Tell your friend that I am at her disposal. I will serve her to the best of my ability.

JACQUELINE. But if that were the case, you understand, that in order to be on the familiar footing of which I speak, the confidant should be seen elsewhere than in the reception-room, is it not true? You understand that his place must be at the table and in the drawing-room. You understand that discretion is a virtue too important to be ignored, but that, aside from good-will, a little skill in management would do no harm. Some evening, like this evening, for example, if it should be pleasant, he must find the latchstring out, and bring some trifling little thing on the sly, like a bold smuggler. No air of mystery must be allowed to betray his cleverness, he must be prudent, wise, and cautious; he must bear in mind this Spanish proverb which leads those that follow it a great ways: "God helps those who help themselves."

FORTUNIO. I beg of you to make use of me.

JACQUELINE. All these conditions being filled, however little one were sure of silence, one might tell the confidant the name of his new friend. He would then receive without any scruple, cleverly as a young soubrette, a purse which he would know how to use. Quick! I perceive Madelon bringing my cloak. Be discreet and prudent. Farewell. The friend is I; the confidant is you; the purse is there at the foot of the chair.

(Exit Jacqueline. Guillaume and Landry at the door-sill.)

GUILLAUME. Hallo! Fortunio; M. André is calling you.

LANDRY. There is some work upon your desk; what are you doing there, out of the office?

FORTUNIO. Hey? I beg your pardon, what did you say? What do you want of me?

GUILLAUME. We are telling you that our employer is asking for you.

LANDRY. Come here right away; you are wanted. What is the dreamer thinking about?

FORTUNIO. Indeed, that is singular, and this adventure is very strange.

(Exeunt.)

ACT THE SECOND

SCENE I

(A Salon.)

CLAVAROCHE *(before a glass)*. In all conscience, if a man were seriously in love with these fine dames, it would be a pretty affair, and the business of a gay Lothario is, on the whole, a ruinous employment. Sometimes, under the most favorable conditions, a valet scratches at the door and obliges you to sneak away. The woman who is losing her reputation for you only half surrenders herself, and in the midst of the most delightful transports thrusts you into some closet or other. Sometimes it is when a man is in his own quarters, stretched upon a sofa and tired out with the drill, that a messenger, dispatched in haste, comes to remind him that somebody a mile away is sighing for him. Quick! a barber, the valet! You run, you fly; there's no time to lose; the husband has returned; it is raining; you must stand waiting for an hour. Think of being ill, or even out of sorts! Not a bit of it; heat, cold, tempest, uncertainty, danger, all that tends to make you a jolly fellow. The difficulty is in possession, but these obstacles have the privilege of enhancing pleasure, and the north wind would be angry if, in cutting your face, it didn't believe it was giving you courage. In truth, love is represented with wings and a quiver; it would be better to paint him as a hunter of wild ducks, with an impervious jacket, and a wig of curled wool to shield the back of his head. What fools men are, to deny themselves their full meals to run after what, pray tell? After the shadow of their pride! But the garrison lasts six months; one can't always go to the café; the comedians of the province bore one; you look at yourself in the glass, and you don't wish to be handsome for nothing. Jacqueline has a fine figure; and so you possess your soul in patience, and accommodate yourself to circumstances without being too particular.

(Enter Jacqueline.)

CLAVAROCHE. Well, my dear, what have you been doing? Did you follow my advice, and are we out of danger?
JACQUELINE. Yes.

CLAVAROCHE. How did you manage it? Tell me all about it. Is it one of M. André's clerks who has charged himself with our salvation?

JACQUELINE. Yes.

CLAVAROCHE. You're a peerless woman, and nobody has more spirit than you. You had the young man come to your boudoir, I suppose. I imagine I can see him now, twirling his hat in his hands. But what story did you tell him in order to succeed so quickly?

JACQUELINE. The first that came to mind; I don't remember.

CLAVAROCHE. Just see how it is with us, and what poor devils we are, when it pleases you to pull the wool over our eyes! And our husband, how does he view the matter? Does the bolt which threatens us already feel the magnetic needle, and begin to turn?

JACQUELINE. Yes.

CLAVAROCHE. Zounds! we shall be amused, and it will be as good as a play to watch this comedy, to observe the attitudes and gestures, and play my own part in it. And the humble slave, if you please, since I saw you, is he already in love with you? I'll bet I met him as I was coming in a business air and appearance about him. Is he already installed in his place, and does he acquit himself of his indispensable duties with some facility? Does he already wear your colors? Does he place the screen before the fire? Has he ventured a few timid words of love and respectful tenderness? Are you pleased with him?

JACQUELINE. Yes.

CLAVAROCHE. And, as a partial payment for future services, have these beautiful, bright, fiery eyes already allowed him to divine that he is permitted to sigh for them, and has he already obtained some favor? Come, frankly, how are you getting on? Have you exchanged looks, have you crossed swords? It is the least you can do to encourage him for the service which he is rendering us.

JACQUELINE. Yes.

CLAVAROCHE. What's the matter with you? You are pensive, and you answer in monosyllables.

JACQUELINE. I have done what you told me to.

CLAVAROCHE. Have you any regret for it?

JACQUELINE. No.

CLAVAROCHE. But you have an anxious air, and something is troubling you.

JACQUELINE. No.

CLAVAROCHE. Do you see anything serious in this kind of pleasantry? Nonsense! there's no harm in it.

JACQUELINE. If people were to know what is going on, why should they say that I am wrong, and perhaps that you are right?

CLAVAROCHE. Nonsense! it's a game, it's a trifle. Don't you love me, Jacqueline?

JACQUELINE. Yes.

CLAVAROCHE. Very well, then! What do you care? Wasn't it to protect our love that you have done what you have?

JACQUELINE. Yes.

CLAVAROCHE. I assure you that it amuses me, and I am not so particular.

JACQUELINE. Hush! it is almost dinner time, and here comes M. André.

CLAVAROCHE. Is that our man who is with him?

JACQUELINE. It is he. My husband invited him, and he is staying here this evening.

(Enter M. André and Fortunio.)

ANDRÉ. No, I don't wish to hear a word of business to-day. I wish every one to enjoy himself and be merry. I am delighted, I am overwhelmed with joy, and I only intend to dine well.

CLAVAROCHE. Dear me! it seems to me that you are in a good humor, M. André.

ANDRÉ. I must tell you all that happened to me yesterday. I suspected my wife unjustly; I had a trap set in front of my garden gate, and I found my cat in it this morning. It served me right, I deserved it. But I want to do justice to Jacqueline, and that you should learn from me that our peace is made and she has forgiven me.

JACQUELINE. All right; I bear no ill-will. Oblige me my saying no more about it.

ANDRÉ. No, I want everybody to know it. I told it all over town, and I have brought home a little sugar Napoleon in my pocket; I am going to put it upon my mantelpiece in sign of reconciliation, and every time I look at it I shall love my wife a hundred times more for it.

CLAVAROCHE. That's acting like a worthy husband; I recognize that, M. André.

ANDRÉ. Captain, I salute you. Will you take dinner with us? We are having a sort of a little merry-making here to-day, and you are welcome.

CLAVAROCHE. You pay me too much honor.

ANDRÉ. Let me present to you a new guest; he is one of my clerks, Captain. Ha! ha! *cedant arma togæ*? Let arms yield to the gown. It is not for the purpose of insulting you; the young rogue has some wit; he is making love to my wife.

CLAVAROCHE. May I ask you your name, sir? I am delighted to know you.

(Fortunio bows.)

ANDRÉ. Fortunio. It's a fortunate name. To tell the truth, he has been working in my office for almost a year, and I didn't observe all the merit that he has. I believe, indeed, that but for Jacqueline I should never have thought of it. His writing is not very neat; and he does some things which are not exempt from reproach; but my wife has need of him for some little matters, and she speaks very highly of his zeal. It is their secret; we husbands don't meddle with these things. An agreeable guest in a small city, is not a thing to be despised; therefore God grant that he be pleased here! We will receive him as well as possible.

FORTUNIO. I shall do my best to be worthy.

ANDRÉ *(to Clavaroche)*. My work, as you know, keeps me busy during the week. I am not sorry to have Jacqueline amuse herself without me as she wishes to. She sometimes needs an arm to walk in the town; the doctor wants her to walk, and the open air is good for her. This young man knows what is going on; he reads aloud very well; he is, moreover, of good family, and his parents have brought him up well; he is a cavalier for my wife, and I ask your friendship for him.

CLAVAROCHE. My friendship, my dear M. André, is entirely at his service; it is something which has been acquired by you and of which you have the disposal.

FORTUNIO. Captain Clavaroche is very kind; and I know not how to thank him.

CLAVAROCHE. Give me your hand! The honor is mine, if you count me among your friends.

ANDRÉ. Come, that's well said! Long live joy! Dinner is waiting for us; give your arm to Jacqueline, and come and taste my wine.

CLAVAROCHE *(low to Jacqueline)*. M. André doesn't appear to me to look at things altogether as I expected.

24

JACQUELINE *(low)*. His confidence and his jealousy depend upon a word and a breath of wind.

CLAVAROCHE *(the same)*. But that is not what you want. If things take this turn, we do not want your clerk.

JACQUELINE *(the same)*. I did what you told me to.

(Exeunt.)

SCENE II

(André's office. Guillaume and Landry, working.)

GUILLAUME. It seems to me that Fortunio left the office very early.

LANDRY. There's a party at the house this evening, and André invited him.

GUILLAUME. Yes, so that the work remains for us. My right arm is paralyzed.

LANDRY. And besides, he's only third clerk. He might have invited us too.

GUILLAUME. After all, he is a good fellow; there's no great harm in that.

LANDRY. No; neither would there have been if we had been invited to the party.

GUILLAUME. H'm, h'm! how good the cooking smells! They're making a racket up there—you can't hear yourself think.

LANDRY. I think they're dancing; I saw some fiddlers.

GUILLAUME. To the devil with these papers! I sha'n't do anything more to-day.

LANDRY. Do you know one thing? I have an idea that something mysterious is going on here!

GUILLAUME. Bah! What is it?

LANDRY. Yes, yes. Everything isn't clear, and if I could gossip a little …

GUILLAUME. Have no fear; I will say nothing about it.

LANDRY. You remember that I saw a man scale the window the other night. Who it was, nobody knew. But to-day, this very evening, I saw something, I am telling you, and what it was I know very well.

GUILLAUME. What was it? Tell me about it.

LANDRY. I saw Jacqueline, in the dusk of the evening, open the garden gate. A man was behind it, who stole along the wall, and who kissed her hand; after that he ran away, and I heard him say to her, "Never fear, I shall be back presently."

GUILLAUME. Indeed! That isn't possible.

LANDRY. I saw him as plainly as I see you.

GUILLAUME. Faith, if that was so, I know what I should do if I were in your place. I should report it to M. André, as you did before, nothing more nor less.

LANDRY. That needs reflection. With a man like M. André, you take your chances. He changes his mind every morning.

GUILLAUME. Do hear the racket they are making! Pish, how the doors slam! Clip-clap, the plates, the dishes, the knives and forks, the bottles! I believe I hear singing.

LANDRY. Yes, it's the voice of M. André himself. Poor simple soul! they will laugh well at him.

GUILLAUME. Come and take a little walk; we can talk at our ease. Faith, when the master is enjoying himself, the least the clerks can do is to take a rest.

(Exeunt.)

SCENE III

(The dining-room. M. André, Clavaroche, Fortunio and Jacqueline, seated at the table.)

CLAVAROCHE. Come, M. Fortunio, give madame something to drink.

FORTUNIO. With all my heart, Captain, and I drink to your health!

CLAVAROCHE. For shame! you are not gallant. To the health of your neighbor.

ANDRÉ. Ah, yes—to the health of my wife. I am delighted, Captain, that you find this wine to your taste. *(He sings.)*

Friends, drink, drink, without ceasing ...

CLAVAROCHE. That song is too old. Sing something, M. Fortunio.

FORTUNIO. If madame wishes it.

ANDRÉ. Ha, ha! the boy knows his audience.

26

JACQUELINE. Oh, yes! sing, if you please.

CLAVAROCHE. One moment. Before singing, eat a little of this cracker; that will clear your throat and give you the high notes.

ANDRÉ. The Captain is joking.

FORTUNIO. Thank you; that would choke me.

CLAVAROCHE. Nonsense! Ask madame to give you a morsel. I am sure that from her fair hand it would appear easy enough to you. *(He looks under the table.)* O heavens! what do I see? Your feet upon the floor! Allow somebody to bring you a cushion, madame.

FORTUNIO *(rising)*. Here is one under this chair. *(He places it under Jacqueline's feet.)*

CLAVAROCHE. That's right, M. Fortunio, I thought you were going to allow me to do it. A young man who is making love ought not to allow any one to anticipate him.

ANDRÉ. Oh, ho! the boy will make his way in the world; you have only to give him a hint.

CLAVAROCHE. Now, then, sing, if you please; we are listening with all our ears.

FORTUNIO. I don't dare to before such critics. I don't know any table songs.

CLAVAROCHE. Since madame has commanded it, you can't get out of it.

FORTUNIO. I will do the best I can then.

CLAVAROCHE. Haven't you addressed any verses to madame yet, M. Fortunio? Come, the occasion presents itself.

ANDRÉ. Silence! silence! Let him sing.

CLAVAROCHE. A love-song above all things isn't it so, M. Fortunio? Nothing else, I beseech you. Madame, request him to sing us a love-song, if you please. I can't live without that.

JACQUELINE. I beg of you, Fortunio.

FORTUNIO *(sings)*.

> If you think that I would tell
> Whom to love I dare,
> No gift so great would me compel
> To name my lady fair.
>
> Join me in singing o'er and o'er
> This very sweet refrain:
> Long live the lady I adore,
> Blond as the ripened grain.

I do what e'er her fancy wills,
She only need command,
And I'll bestow the love that thrills,
Yea, life, with heart and hand.

By the woe, which love confers,
Where misery draws breath,
My soul is true and nobly bears
Its burden unto death.

Ah, too well, I love to tell
Who is my heart's desire,
But rather than her name I'd spell,
I'd willingly expire.

ANDRÉ. In truth, the sly dog is in love, as he says; he has tears in his eyes. Here, my boy, take a drink to recover yourself. It must be some pretty shop-girl of the town who has done you that ill turn.

CLAVAROCHE. I don't believe that M. Fortunio has such a vulgar ambition as that; his song is worthy of something better than a pretty shop-girl. What does madame say about it, and what is her opinion?

JACQUELINE. Very good! Give me your arm, and let us go and take some coffee.

CLAVAROCHE. Quick, M. Fortunio, offer your arm to madame.

JACQUELINE *(takes Fortunio's arm. Low, as she goes out).* Did you do my errand?

FORTUNIO. Yes, madame; everything is in the office.

JACQUELINE. Go, and wait for me in my chamber; I will join you there presently.

(Exeunt.)

SCENE IV

(Jacqueline's chamber. Fortunio enters.)

FORTUNIO. How can there be any happier man than I? I am certain that Jacqueline loves me, and by all the signs that she has given me, I can't be mistaken about it. Already I am received with open arms,

28

entertained, petted in the house. She has seated me beside her at the table; if she goes for a walk, I go with her. What sweetness! what a voice! what a smile! When she fixes her gaze upon me, I don't know whether I am on my head or my feet; I am speechless with joy. I should fall upon her neck if I didn't restrain myself. No; ... the more I think of it the more I consider it, the least signs, the slightest favors, all is certain; she loves me, she loves me, and I should be a downright fool if I were to pretend not to see it. When I was singing just now, how I saw her eyes shine! Come, lose no time. Place here this box which contains some jewels; it is a private commission; and surely, Jacqueline will not be long in coming.

(Enter Jacqueline.)

JACQUELINE. Are you there, Fortunio?

FORTUNIO. Yes. Here is your box of jewels, madame, the one you wanted me to get for you.

JACQUELINE. You are a man of your word, and I am delighted with you.

FORTUNIO. How can I tell you how I feel? A look from your eyes has changed my fate, and I live only to serve you.

JACQUELINE. That was a pretty song that you sang for us at table just now. For whom was it composed? Will you give me a copy of it?

FORTUNIO. It was composed for you, madame. I am dying of love, and my life is in your hands. *(He drops upon his knees.)*

JACQUELINE. Indeed! I thought that your refrain forbade your saying whom you love.

FORTUNIO. Ah, Jacqueline, have pity upon me. My suffering does not date from yesterday. For two years have I followed the trace of your footsteps through these walks. For two years, without your ever having known of my existence perhaps, you have never gone out or in, your light and trembling shadow has not appeared behind your curtains, you have not opened your window, you have not breathed a breath of air, that I was not there, that I have not seen you. I could not approach you, but your beauty, thank God, belonged to me as the sunshine belongs to us all; I sought it, I breathed it, I lived upon the shadow of your life. Did you pass the morning at the garden gate, I returned there in the evening to weep. A few words dropped from your lips, if they came to my ears, were repeated by me the live-long day. Did you cultivate flowers, my chamber was filled with them. Did you sing at the piano of an evening, I knew your romances by heart. All that you loved, I loved; I was intoxicated by whatever passed your lips or entered your mind. Alas! I see that you smile. God knows that my suffering is real, and that I love you to death!

JACQUELINE. I am not smiling because I hear you say that you have loved me for two years, but I am smiling because of what I think, that it will be two days to-morrow.

FORTUNIO. May I die if truth is not as dear to me as my love, and if it is not two years that I have existed only for you.

JACQUELINE. Get up right away. If anybody were to come, what would they think of me?

FORTUNIO. No, I won't get up I won't leave this position, if you won't believe my words. If you reject my love, at least do not doubt of it.

JACQUELINE. Is this some enterprise that you are engaged in?

FORTUNIO. An enterprise full of fear, full of misery and of hope. I do not know whether I am dead or alive; how I have dared to speak to you, I do not know. I have lost my reason. I love, I suffer; you must know it, you must see it, you must pity me!

JACQUELINE. Is this bad, obstinate child going to remain there an hour? Come, get up; I wish it.

FORTUNIO. Do you believe that I love you?

JACQUELINE. No, I do not believe it; this makes me less ready to believe it.

FORTUNIO. It's impossible! you can't doubt it.

JACQUELINE. Bah, one doesn't get on so fast at three words of gallantry.

FORTUNIO. For God's sake, just look at me! Who could have taught me deception? I am nothing but a child, and I have never been in love with anybody in my life, if it isn't with you who are ignorant of it.

JACQUELINE. You make love to pretty shop-girls. I know it as well as if I had seen it.

FORTUNIO. You are jesting. Who could have told you such a thing?

JACQUELINE. Yes, yes; you go to dances and picnics.

FORTUNIO. With my friends, of a Sunday. What harm is there in that?

JACQUELINE. I said as much to you yesterday, that is easily accounted for. You are young, and at the age when the heart is light one doesn't count the cost.

FORTUNIO. What can I do to convince you? Tell me, I beseech you.

JACQUELINE. You want a pretty counselor. Very well, you must prove it.

FORTUNIO. Good heavens! I have only tears. Do tears prove that one loves? What! you see me on my knees before you; my heart is ready to burst; the thing that has cast me at your feet is a sorrow which is crushing me, that I have struggled against for two years, that I can no longer bear, and you remain cold and incredulous! Can I not impart to you a single spark of the fire which is consuming me? You even deny that I am suffering, when I am ready to die before your eyes? Ah, it is more cruel than a refusal! It is more terrible than contempt! Indifference itself might believe, and I have not deserved this.

JACQUELINE. Get up somebody is coming! I believe you, I love you. Go down by the back staircase; return to the parlor; I will be there. *(Exit.)*

FORTUNIO *(alone)*. She loves me! Jacqueline loves me! She goes away, she leaves me like this! No, I can't go down yet. Hush! somebody is coming; somebody has stopped her; they are coming here. I must hurry out of here! *(He raises the portière.)* Ah, the door is locked on the outside; I can't get out. What shall I do? If I go out the other way, I shall run against whoever is coming.

CLAVAROCHE *(outside)*. Come on; come for a little while,

FORTUNIO. It's the Captain who is coming up with her. I must hide myself quickly, and wait; they mustn't find me here.

(He hides himself in the depths of the alcove. Enter Clavaroche and Jacqueline.)

CLAVAROCHE *(throwing himself upon a sofa)*. Zounds! Madame, I have been looking for you everywhere. What were you doing all by yourself?

JACQUELINE *(aside)*. Praise God, Fortunio has gone!

CLAVAROCHE. You leave me in a situation which bores me to death. What use have I for André, if you please? And really you leave us together when the convivial wine of the husband would render more acceptable the agreeable conversation of the wife.

FORTUNIO *(concealed)*. This is singular. What does this mean?

CLAVAROCHE *(opening the jewel box upon the table)*. Let us see. Are these rings? And what are you going to do with them, pray tell? Are you making somebody a present?

JACQUELINE. You know very well it is a part of our little ruse.

31

CLAVAROCHE. But, my conscience, what a lot of money! If you count upon using the same stratagem every day, our game will end presently by not being worth while ... By the by, how that dinner amused me, and what a curious appearance our young initiate has!

FORTUNIO *(concealed)*. Initiate! What mystery is this? Can it be I that he is talking about?

CLAVAROCHE. The chain is beautiful; it's a little gem. That was a singular idea of yours.

FORTUNIO *(concealed)*. Ah, it seems that he is also in Jacqueline's confidence!

CLAVAROCHE. How the poor boy trembled when he raised his glass! How he entertained me with his cushions, and what fun it was to watch him!

FORTUNIO *(concealed)*. Surely, it is I that he is talking about, and it's the dinner of a little while ago that's in question.

CLAVAROCHE. I suppose you will return this to the jeweler who furnished it?

FORTUNIO *(concealed)*. Return the chain! What for?

CLAVAROCHE. His song delighted me especially, and M. André particularly noticed that; I'll be blessed if he didn't actually have tears in his eyes over it!

FORTUNIO *(concealed)*. I can't yet believe my ears. Is this a dream? Am I awake? What kind of a fellow is this Clavaroche?

CLAVAROCHE. However, it is useless to carry the thing any further. What's the use of a troublesome third party, if suspicions are no longer aroused? These husbands never fail to adore their wives' lovers. You see what has happened! From the moment you are trusted you must get rid of the chandler.

JACQUELINE. Who knows what may happen? With a man like that there is never anything sure, and it is necessary to keep some means at hand for getting out of a scrape.

FORTUNIO *(concealed)*. If they are making a cat's-paw of me, it can't be without a motive. All these speeches are enigmas.

CLAVAROCHE. It's my advice to get rid of him.

JACQUELINE. Just as you please. It is not myself that I am consulting in this affair. If wrong-doing were necessary, do you think it would be from my choice? But who knows if to-morrow—this evening—in an hour—some ill wind won't arise? We can't count upon the calm with too much security.

CLAVAROCHE. Do you think so?

FORTUNIO *(concealed)*. Good heavens! he's her paramour.

CLAVAROCHE. However, do whatever you like about it. Without altogether ousting the young man, you might keep him in working order, but at a little distance, and put him into leading-strings. If M. André's suspicions were ever aroused again, well and good! In that case you would have your M. Fortunio at hand to divert them anew. I take him for an easy prey; he readily rises to bait.

JACQUELINE. I thought somebody moved.

CLAVAROCHE. Yes, I thought I heard a sigh.

JACQUELINE. Probably it was Madelon; she is putting the study to rights.

ACT THE THIRD

SCENE I

(The garden. Enter Jacqueline and the Servant.)

MADELON. Madame, a danger is menacing you. As I was in the arbor just now, I heard M. André talking with one of his clerks. As nearly as I could make out, it pertained to some ambush which would take place to-night.

JACQUELINE. An ambush! Where? For what purpose?

MADELON. In the office. The clerk asserted that he saw you, yourself, madame, and a man with you, in the garden. M. André swore by all that is good and holy that he would take you by surprise and have you prosecuted.

JACQUELINE. Aren't you mistaken, Madelon?

MADELON. Madame will do as she sees fit. I haven't the honor of her confidences; that doesn't prevent a person from rendering a service. My work is waiting for me.

JACQUELINE. That's right, and you may rest assured that I shall not be ungrateful. Have you seen Fortunio this morning? Where is he? I want to speak to him.

MADELON. He hasn't come to the office; the Gardener has seen him, I believe; but they are at a loss to know what has become of him, and they were looking for him all over the garden a while ago. Look! there is M. Guillaume, the head clerk, looking for him again; don't you see him going along there?

GUILLAUME *(behind the scenes)*. Hallo! Fortunio! Fortunio! hallo! Where are you?

JACQUELINE. Go, Madelon, try to find him.

(Exit Madelon. Enter Clavaroche.)

CLAVAROCHE. What the devil is going on here? How is this! I, who have some claims, I think, to M. André's friendship, meet him, and he doesn't greet me; the clerks look at me askance, and I don't know but even the dog wanted to grab me by the heel. What has happened, if you please, and what's the reason for their abusing people?

JACQUELINE. It's no joking matter. Just what I have expected has come to pass, and seriously this time; it is no longer time for words, but for action.

CLAVAROCHE. For action! What do you mean?

JACQUELINE. That these pesky clerks are playing the spy; that we have been seen; that André knows it; that he intends to hide himself in the office, and that we are running the gravest danger.

CLAVAROCHE. Is that all that's troubling you?

JACQUELINE. Certainly; what would you want worse? That we shall escape them to-day, since we are warned, is not the difficulty; but the moment that André acts on the quiet, we have everything to fear from him.

CLAVAROCHE. Really! that is all there is to the affair, and there isn't anything worse than that?

JACQUELINE. Are you crazy? How is it possible for you to joke about it?

CLAVAROCHE. Because there is nothing so simple as for us to get out of the scrape. M. André, you say, is furious? Well, let him bluster; what inconvenience? He wants to put himself in ambush? Let him do so; nothing could be better. Are the clerks of the party? Let them be, with all the town, if it amuses them. They wish to surprise the beautyful Jacqueline and her very humble servant! Ah, let them surprise; I have no objections. What do you see in that to trouble us?

JACQUELINE. I can't understand anything you're talking about.

CLAVAROCHE. Have Fortunio called for me. Where has that fine gentleman hidden his head? What! we are in danger, and the scamp abandons us! Come, notify him.

JACQUELINE. I thought about that. Nobody knows where he is, and he has not appeared this morning.

CLAVAROCHE. Nonsense! that's impossible. He must be somewhere around, not far from your petticoats; you have forgotten him in some closet, and your maid has inadvertently hung him up upon a clothes-hook.

JACQUELINE. But, after all, in what way could he be of use to us? I asked where he was without knowing just why myself. I don't see, upon reflection, what good he can be to us.

CLAVAROCHE. Hey! Don't you see that I am preparing myself to make to him the greatest of sacrifices no less a matter than to cede to him for this evening all the privileges of love?

JACQUELINE. For this evening? And for what purpose?

CLAVAROCHE. For the positive and express purpose that worthy M. André may not uselessly pass a night in the open air. You wouldn't wish for these poor clerks, who are going to render good for evil, to find nobody at hand? For shame! we mustn't allow these good people to remain empty-handed; we must send them somebody.

JACQUELINE. That shall not be done. Find something else; that is a horrible idea of yours, and I can't consent to it.

CLAVAROCHE. Why horrible? Nothing is more harmless. You write a word to Fortunio, if you can't find him yourself; for the least little word in the world is better than the longest book. You have him come this evening, under pretext of a rendezvous. He comes; the clerks take him by surprise, and M. André seizes him by the collar, What is your pleasure concerning him? Thereupon you go down in dishabille, and demand why they are making such a noise, the most naturally in the world. They explain it to you. M. André, in furor, demands of you in turn why his young clerk crawls into his garden. You blush a little at first, then you openly confess all that it pleases you to confess: that this boy visits the shop for you; that he brings parcels for you secretly; in short, the truth pure and simple. What is so terrifying in that?

JACQUELINE. They wouldn't believe me. A pretty likelihood that I should grant clandestine meetings to settle accounts.

CLAVAROCHE. People always believe the truth. Truth has a ring impossible not to recognize, and high-born natures are never deceived by it. Is it not, in truth, for your commissions that you employ this young man?

JACQUELINE. Yes.

CLAVAROCHE. Well, then! since you do that, you can say so, and they will see it plainly enough. Let him have the proof in his pocket, a jewel box, like yesterday; the first thing at hand will suffice. Consider that, if we don't employ this means, we shall be bothered for the whole year. M. André will spy on us to-night, tomorrow night, and so on until he discovers us. The less he finds, the more he will search; but let him find something once for all, and we are free of it.

JACQUELINE. That is impossible! It isn't to be thought of.

CLAVAROCHE. A secret meeting in a garden, moreover, is no great sin, strictly speaking. If you fear the air, you have only to stay in your room. They will find nobody but the young man, and he will get out of the scrape some way. It would be ridiculous if a woman couldn't prove that she is innocent when she is. Come, your writing tablet, and here is a pencil for you.

JACQUELINE. You don't mean it, Clavaroche! This is a willful injury that you are doing.

CLAVAROCHE *(presenting her with pencil and paper).* Now write, if you please: "At midnight, to-night, in the garden."

JACQUELINE. It is sending that child into a trap; it is delivering him to the enemy.

CLAVAROCHE. Don't sign it; it's useless. *(He takes the paper.)* Frankly, my dear, the night will be cool, and you had better remain in your room. Let the young man take his walk by himself, and profit by his experience. I think, like you, that one would have difficulty in believing that it is on account of your merchants that he comes. You would do better, if anybody questions you, to say that you are ignorant of everything, and that you will have nothing to do with the matter.

JACQUELINE. This specimen of my handwriting will be a proof.

CLAVAROCHE. Tush! do you think that we men of courage ever show a husband any of his wife's writing? What would we gain by it? Should we be less culpable if a crime were to be shared? Moreover, you know that your hand doubtless trembled a little, and the handwriting is almost disguised. Nonsense! I am going to give this letter to the Gardener; Fortunio will have it directly. Come along; the vultures have their prey, and the bird of Venus, the pale turtle-dove, may sleep peacefully upon her nest.

(Exeunt.)

SCENE II

(A beech grove.)

FORTUNIO *(alone, seated upon the grass).* To cause a young man to fall in love with her, for the sole purpose of diverting suspicions to him which have fallen upon another; to lead him to believe that she loves him, to tell him so in case of need; to disturb, perhaps, many tranquil nights; to fill with doubt and hope a heart young and willing to suffer; to cast a stone into a lake which has never before had a ripple upon its surface; to expose a man to suspicion, to all the

dangers of blissful love, and yet accord him nothing; to remain un-
moved and lifeless in an act of life and death; to deceive, to lie—to
lie heartlessly; to make her person an enticement; to trifle with
everything sacred under the heavens, like a thief with loaded dice—
these are the things that make a woman smile! these are the things
she does, with a little air of abstraction. *(He rises.)* It is your first
experience, Fortunio, in the apprenticeship of the world. Think,
reflect, compare, examine, do not judge hastily. That woman there
has a lover whom she adores; she is suspected, tormented, threatened; she is frightened; she is about to lose the man who fills her life,
who is more to her than all the world. Her husband is suddenly
aroused, warned by a spy; he awakens her; he wants to drag her to a
court of justice. Her family will disown her, an entire community
will condemn her; her character is ruined and dishonored, and yet
she loves and can not cease from loving. She must save the sole
object of her solicitude, of her anguish, and of her distress; she must
love in order to continue to live, and she must deceive in order to
love. She leans upon her window-sill; she sees a young man down
below; who is it? She doesn't know him; she has never seen his face;
is he good, or wicked; is he discreet, or treacherous; tenderhearted,
or thoughtless? She knows nothing about him; she has need of him;
she calls him; she signals to him; she adds a flower to her adorn-
ment; she speaks; she has staked the happiness of her life upon a
card, and she plays at *rouge et noir*. If she had but addressed herself
to Guillaume instead of me, what would have come of it? Guillaume
is a good fellow, but he has never perceived that his heart serves him
for any other purpose than beating. Guillaume would have been
delighted to go and dine with his employer, to be seated beside
Jacqueline at table, just as I was delighted myself; but he would have
seen nothing further in it; he would have fallen in love only with M.
André's wine-cellar; he would not have thrown himself upon his
knees; he would not have listened at the doors; it would have been
for him all profit. What harm would there have been, then, for her to
use him without his knowledge, to divert the suspicions of a husband? None whatever. He would have peacefully played the part
that was required of him; he would have lived happily, tranquilly,
ten years without ever perceiving it. Jacqueline also would have
been happy, tranquil, ten years without saying a word to him. She
would have flirted with him, and he would have responded to her;
but no harm would have come of it. Everything would have gone on

capitally, and nobody need to have worried over the day when mur-
der would out. *(He sits down again.)* Why did she address herself to
me? Was she aware that I loved her? Why to me rather than to
Guillaume? Was it chance, or was it calculation? Perhaps deep down
in her heart she suspected that I was not indifferent. Could she have
seen me at that window? Had she ever turned of an evening, when I
was observing her in the garden? But if she knew that I loved her,
why then? Because that love rendered her project easier, and I was
going at the first word to fall into the trap that she was setting for
me. My love was only a lucky circumstance; she saw nothing in it
but an opportunity. Is that altogether certain? Isn't there anything
besides that? What! she sees that I am suffering, and she thinks only
of profiting by it! What! she finds me upon her footsteps, love in my
heart, desire in my eyes, young and ardent, ready to die for her, and
when, seeing me at her feet, she smiles upon me and tells me that
she loves me, it is a cold-blooded calculation, and nothing more!
Nothing of truth in that smile, in that hand which agitates mine, in
the sound of the voice which intoxicates me? O, God! if that be so,
with what a monster am I dealing, and into what an abyss have I
fallen. *(He rises.)* No; so much horror isn't possible! No; a woman
can not be a malignant statue, at the same time alive and frozen! No;
if I were to see it with my own eyes, if I were to hear it from her
own lips, I should never believe in any such a thing as that. No;
when she smiled upon me, it wasn't because she loved me, but she
smiled to see that I loved her. When she gave me her hand, she
didn't give me her heart, but she allowed me to give mine. When she
said to me, "I love you," she meant to say, "Love me." No, Jacqueline
is not wicked; there is nothing of calculation or coldness about her.
She lies, she deceives, she is a woman; she is coquettish, addicted to
raillery, joyous, audacious, but not base, not heartless. Ah, fool that
you are, you love her! you love her! You implore, you weep, and she
laughs at you!

(Enter Madelon.)

MADELON. Ah, thank heavens! I have found you at last. Madame
is asking for you; she is in her chamber. Come right away; she is
waiting for you.

FORTUNIO. Do you know what she wants of me? I can't go just now.

MADELON. Have you some business with the trees? She is greatly troubled—go! The whole household is up in arms.

THE GARDENER *(entering).* Here you are, sir. I have been looking for you everywhere. There is a note for you, which our mistress gave me a while ago.

FORTUNIO *(reading).* "At midnight, tonight, in the garden." *(Aloud.)* Is this from Jacqueline?

THE GARDENER. Yes, sir. Is there any reply to it?

GUILLAUME *(entering).* What are you doing, Fortunio? You are wanted in the office.

FORTUNIO. I'm coming—I'm coming. *(Low to Madelon.)* What was it you were saying just now? What trouble is your mistress in?

MADELON *(low).* It's a secret. M. André is angry.

FORTUNIO *(the same).* He is angry? What about?

MADELON *(the same).* He has taken it into his head that madame was receiving somebody on the sly. You won't say anything about it, will you? He is going to hide himself to-night in the office. It is I who discovered that, and if I tell it to you well, it's because I think that you are not unconcerned in it.

FORTUNIO. Why hide himself in the office?

MADELON. To discover everything and sue for a divorce.

FORTUNIO. Indeed! is it possible?

THE GARDENER. Is there any reply, sir?

FORTUNIO. I am going to see her myself. Come, let us go.

(Exeunt.)

SCENE III

(A chamber. Jacqueline.)

JACQUELINE *(alone).* No, that must not be done. Who knows what a man like André, once driven to violence, might invent to be revenged? I shall not send that young man into such a frightful danger. That Clavaroche is pitiless; everything is a battle-field to him, and he hasn't any mercy for anything or anybody. What's the use of exposing Fortunio, since there is nothing so simple as not to expose him, or anybody else. I believe that every suspicion would be banished by this means, but the means itself is an injury, and I won't

41

employ it. No, that pains and displeases me. I don't wish that boy to be abused; since he says that he loves me, well and good I have no objection; I don't return evil for good.

(Enter Fortunio.)

JACQUELINE. Did you receive a note from me, and have you read it?

FORTUNIO. I did receive it, and I have read it. I am at your service.

JACQUELINE. It isn't necessary. I have changed my mind. Tear up the note, and say no more about it.

FORTUNIO. Can I be of any other service to you?

JACQUELINE *(aside).* It is strange he doesn't insist. *(Aloud.)* No, indeed, I have no need of you. I asked you for your song.

FORTUNIO. Here it is. Is that all?

JACQUELINE. Yes I think so. What's the matter with you? It seems to me that you are pale.

FORTUNIO. If you don't need me, madame, permit me to withdraw.

JACQUELINE. I like this song very much; it has a little artless air which is in keeping with you, and you have composed it very well.

FORTUNIO. You are very kind.

JACQUELINE. Yes, you see, at first I had an idea of having you come; but then I reflected it would be madness; I listened to you too readily. Sit down at the piano, and sing your little song for me.

FORTUNIO. Excuse me, I can not now.

JACQUELINE. Why not? Are you suffering, or is it a naughty whim? I have a good mind to make you sing whether you want to or not. Haven't I some right of proprietorship over this sheet of paper? *(She places the song upon the piano.)*

FORTUNIO. It isn't because of unwillingness. I can't stay any longer, and M. André needs me.

JACQUELINE. I don't care if you may be scolded; sit down there and sing.

FORTUNIO. If you exact it, I obey. *(He sits down.)*

JACQUELINE. Well, what are you thinking about? Are you waiting for somebody to come?

FORTUNIO. I am suffering. Do not detain me.

JACQUELINE. Sing first; we will see afterward if you are suffering, and whether I will detain you or not. Sing, I tell you; I want you to. Won't you sing? Well, what's the reason? Come, let me see. If you will sing, I will give you a penny.

FORTUNIO. See here, Jacqueline—listen to me. You would have done better to tell me all about it, and I would have consented to everything.

JACQUELINE. What do you mean? What are you talking about?

FORTUNIO. Yes, you would have done better to tell me. Yes, I swear it, I would have done everything for you!

JACQUELINE. Done everything for me? What do you mean by that?

FORTUNIO. Ah, Jacqueline, Jacqueline, you must love him very much! It must cost you something to lie to me and mock me so unmercifully.

JACQUELINE. I mock you? Who told you so?

FORTUNIO. Don't lie any more, I beg of you; this will do. I know everything.

JACQUELINE. In short, what do you know?

FORTUNIO. I was in your chamber yesterday when Clavaroche was there.

JACQUELINE. Is it possible? Were you in the alcove?

FORTUNIO. Yes, I was there; for heaven's sake, don't say a word about it.

(A silence.)

JACQUELINE. Since you know everything, sir, it only remains for me now to beg you to be silent. I am too well aware of my wrongs toward you to wish even to make the attempt of softening them in your eyes. That which necessity compels, and that to which it might lead, another than you might perhaps understand, and would be able, if not to forgive, at least to excuse my conduct; but you are, unfortunately, a party too much interested to judge of it with indulgence. I am resigned, and I await your pleasure.

FORTUNIO. Have no kind of fear whatever. If I were to do anything which could injure you in the least, I would cut off my right hand.

JACQUELINE. Your word is sufficient, and I have no right to doubt it. I should say, even, that if you were to forget it, I should have still less right to complain of it. My imprudence ought to bear the penalty. It was without knowing you, sir, that I addressed myself to you. If that circumstance renders my fault less, it renders my danger greater. Since I have exposed myself to it, treat me as you think fit. It might be worth while to explain some words exchanged

43

yesterday. Not being able to justify everything, I would rather keep silent about all. Let me believe that your pride is the only thing injured. If that is so, it will be forgotten in two days; later on we will speak of it again.

FORTUNIO. Never; it is the wish of my heart.

JACQUELINE. As you like; I must obey. If I am not to see you again, however, I should have one word to add. Between you and me, I have no fear, since you have promised me to be silent; but there exists another person whose presence in this house might have unpleasant consequences.

FORTUNIO. I have nothing to say on that subject.

JACQUELINE. I demand of you to listen to me. A clash between you and him—you must feel it —would be my ruin. I will do anything to prevent it. Whatever you exact, I submit to it without a murmur. Do not leave me without reflecting upon it; dictate the conditions yourself. Must the person of whom I speak keep away from here for a time? Is it necessary for him to offer you an apology? Whatever you shall judge suitable will be received by me as a favor, and by him as a duty. The recollection of certain pleasantries obliges me to interrogate you upon this point. What do you decide? Answer me.

FORTUNIO. I exact nothing. You love him; be at rest so long as he loves you.

JACQUELINE. I thank you for these two promises. If you should ever repent of them, I repeat that every condition imposed by you will be met. Count upon my gratitude. May I from now on repair my wrongs in any other way? Is there any means of obliging you at my disposal? What though you will not believe me, I declare to you that I would do everything in the world to leave with you a less disadvantageous memory of me. What can I do? I am at your orders.

FORTUNIO. Nothing. Farewell, madame. Have no fear; you will never have to complain concerning me. *(He starts to leave, and takes his song.)*

JACQUELINE. Ah, Fortunio, leave me that.

FORTUNIO. What would you do with it, cruel creature that you are? You have been talking to me for a quarter of an hour, and not one kind word has fallen from your lips. The question in point pertains to your excuses, to sacrifices and reparations, to your Clava-roche and his senseless vanity, to my pride! Do you think that you have wounded it? Do you believe that the thing which troubles me is to have been taken for a dupe, and made sport of at a dinner? I simply remember nothing about that. When I tell you that I love you, do you believe that I do not feel it? When I talk to you of two years of suffering, do you think that I am doing as you do? What! you break my heart; you pretend that you repent of it, and this is the way that you forsake me! Necessity, you say, made you commit a fault, and you are sorry for it; you are blushing; you turn away your head; my suffering excites your pity; you see me, you understand your act; and this is the way that you heal the wound that you have made! Ah, it is of the heart, Jacqueline, and you have only to stretch out your hand. I swear to you, if you had but wished it, as shameful as it is to say it, although you will laugh at it yourself, I was capable of consenting to everything. O, God! my strength is failing me; I can not go away from here. *(He leans upon a table.)*

JACQUELINE. Poor boy! I am to blame. Here, breathe this vial.

FORTUNIO. Ah, keep them, keep them for him, these attentions of which I am unworthy; it isn't for me that they are made. I haven't an inventive mind; I am neither felicitous nor clever; I can not, upon occasion, invent a profound stratagem. Fool that I am! I thought that I was loved; because you smiled upon me; because your hand trembled in mine; because your eyes appeared to seek my eyes and to invite me like two angels to a feast of joy and life; because your lips were parted, and a heavenly sound fell from them. Yes, I confess I have been dreaming. I thought that it was thus a person loved! What a calamity! Was it at a parade that your smile felicitated me upon the beauty of my horse? Was it the sunlight darting across my helmet which dazzled your eyes? I came from a dark room, whence I had followed for two years your walks along a foot-path. I was a poor clerk who had taken it upon himself to weep in silence. That was a fine thing for anybody to love!

JACQUELINE. Poor boy!

FORTUNIO. Yes, poor boy! Say it again, for I don't know whether I am awake or dreaming, and, after all, whether you don't love me. Since yesterday I have been idle; I have been pondering; I recall what I saw with my eyes, what I heard with my ears, and I demand of myself if it is possible. What have I ever done to you, Jacqueline? How can it be possible, without any motive, without having for me either love or hatred, without knowing me, without ever having seen me—how can it be possible that you, whom everybody loves, whom I have seen dispensing charities and watering these flowers here,

45

who are good, who believe in God, to whom never ... Ah! I am accusing you, you whom I love more than my life! O, heavens! have I reproached you? Jacqueline, forgive me!

JACQUELINE. Calm yourself; come, calm yourself.

FORTUNIO. And what am I good for, great God! if it isn't to give my life to you—if it isn't for the most paltry use which you wish to make of me—if it isn't to follow you, to protect you, to ward off evil from you? I dare to complain, and you had chosen me! My place was at your table; I was of some account to you. You were saying to all the world, to these gardens, these meadows, to smile upon me as you were doing; your beautiful and radiant image was beginning to walk before me, and I followed it; I was beginning to live... Do I have to lose you, Jacqueline? Have I done anything that you should dismiss me? Why won't you still pretend to love me? *(He falls in a faint.)*

JACQUELINE *(running to him)*. My God! what have I done? Fortunio, come to yourself again.

FORTUNIO. Who are you? Let me go.

JACQUELINE. Lean upon me. Come to the window; for mercy's sake; lean upon me; place this arm upon my shoulder, I beg of you, Fortunio.

FORTUNIO. It's nothing. I am all right again.

JACQUELINE. How pale he is! how his heart beats! Won't you bathe your temples? Take this cushion—take this handkerchief. Am I so odious to you that you refuse me that?

FORTUNIO. I am feeling better, thank you.

JACQUELINE. How cold his hands are! Where are you going? You can not go yet. Wait at least a little while. Since I have been the cause of your suffering so much, let me, at least, care for you.

FORTUNIO. It isn't necessary. I must go down. Forgive me for whatever I may have said to you; I was not master of my words.

JACQUELINE. What do you wish me to forgive you? Alas! it is you who do not forgive. But what is your hurry? Why do you leave me? Your eyes are looking for something. Don't you recognize me? Keep quiet, I beseech of you. For my sake, Fortunio, you mustn't go yet.

FORTUNIO. No. Farewell—I can't stay.

JACQUELINE. I have hurt you very much.

FORTUNIO. They were asking for me when I came up here. Farewell, madame; rely upon me.

JACQUELINE. Shall I see you again?

FORTUNIO. If you wish to.

JACQUELINE. Are you coming to the parlor this evening?

FORTUNIO. If you wish to have me.

JACQUELINE. You are going, then? Wait a little longer.

FORTUNIO. Farewell! farewell! I can not stay. *(Exit.)*

JACQUELINE *(calls)*. Fortunio, listen to me.

FORTUNIO *(reentering)*. What do you want of me, Jacqueline?

JACQUELINE. Listen to me; I must speak to you. I don't want to beg your pardon; I don't want to take anything back; I don't want to justify myself. You are good, brave, and sincere; I have been false and disloyal. I don't want to leave you thus.

FORTUNIO. I forgive you with all my heart.

JACQUELINE. No, you are suffering; the harm is done. Where are you going? What are you going to do? How is it possible, knowing everything, that you should have come here again?

FORTUNIO. You sent for me.

JACQUELINE. But you came to tell me that I should see you at this rendezvous. Would you have been there?

FORTUNIO. Yes, if it were to render you a service, and I confess to you that I believed it.

JACQUELINE. Why to render me a service?

FORTUNIO. Madelon said a few words ...

JACQUELINE. You knew it, unhappy man, and you were coming to the garden!

FORTUNIO. The first word I ever said to you in my life was that I would willingly die for you, and the second was that I never lied.

JACQUELINE. You knew it, and you were coming? Do you dream of what you are saying? It was a question of an ambush.

FORTUNIO. I knew everything.

JACQUELINE. It was a question of being surprised, of being killed perhaps, dragged into prison; what do I know? It is too horrible to mention.

FORTUNIO. I knew everything.

JACQUELINE. You knew all about it you knew everything? You were hidden there yesterday, in that alcove, behind the curtain. You listened, didn't you? You knew all about that, didn't you?

FORTUNIO. Yes.

JACQUELINE. You know that I lie, that I am deceitful, that I am sporting with you, and that I am killing you? You know that I love Clavaroche, and that he makes me do whatever he pleases; that I am playing a comedy; that there, yesterday, I took you for a dupe; that I am cowardly and despicable; that I am exposing you to death for my pleasure—you knew all this; you were sure of it? Very well, very well ... what do you know now?

FORTUNIO. But, Jacqueline, I believe ... I know ...

JACQUELINE. Do you know that I love you, child that you are; that you must pardon me, or I shall die; and that I demand it of you upon my knees?

SCENE IV

(The dining-room. André, Clavaroche, Fortunio, and Jacqueline at table.)

ANDRÉ. Heaven be praised! here we all are, all happy, all reunited, and all friends. If I ever doubt my wife again, may my wine poison me!

JACQUELINE. Give me a glass of wine, M. Fortunio.

CLAVAROCHE *(low)*. I repeat to you that your clerk bores me. Do me the favor of sending him away.

JACQUELINE. I am doing just what you told me to.

ANDRÉ. When I think that I spent last night in the office, chilling myself to the heart upon a cursed suspicion, I don't know what name to call myself.

JACQUELINE. M. Fortunio, give me that cushion.

CLAVAROCHE *(low)*. Do you take me for a second M. André? If your clerk doesn't leave the house, I shall leave it myself very soon.

JACQUELINE. I am doing just as you told me to.

ANDRÉ. But I have told it to everybody. Justice must be done here upon earth. The whole town shall know who I am; and in future, for penitence, I shall never doubt, whatever it may be.

JACQUELINE. M. Fortunio, I drink to your sweethearts.

CLAVAROCHE *(low)*. Enough of that, Jacqueline; and I understand what that signifies. That isn't what I told you to do.

ANDRÉ. Yes, to Fortunio 's sweethearts! *(He sings.)*

Friends, drink, drink without ceasing ...

FORTUNIO. That song is very old. Sing something, M. Clavaroche!

(End of The Chandler.)

Printed in Great Britain
by Amazon

48133233R00029